...ortant skill... ...at ...ach. The A... ...sy ...d to suppo.. ...you and your child through this process. ...ialists, each book in the series includes carefully selected words and sentence structures to help children advance from beginner to intermediate to proficient readers.

Here are some tips to keep in mind as you read these books with your child:

First, preview the book together. Read the title. Then look at the cover. Ask your child, "What is happening on the cover? What do you think this book is about?"

Next, skim through the pages of the book and look at the illustrations. This will help your child use the illustrations to understand the story.

Then encourage your child to read. If he or she stumbles over words, try some of these strategies:

- **use the pictures as clues**
- **point out words that are repeated**
- **sound out difficult words**
- **break up bigger words into smaller chunks**
- **use the context to lend meaning**

Finally, find out if your child understands what he or she is reading. After you have finished reading, ask, "What happened in this book?"

Above all, understand that each child learns to read at a different rate. Make sure to praise your young reader and provide encouragement along the way!

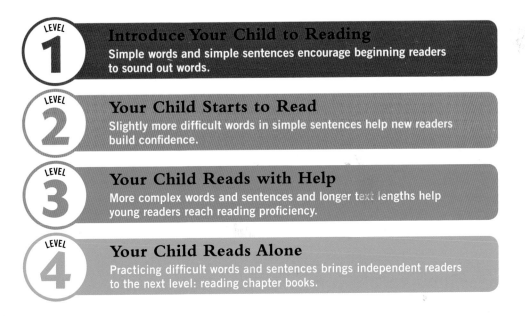

LEVEL 1

Introduce Your Child to Reading
Simple words and simple sentences encourage beginning readers to sound out words.

LEVEL 2

Your Child Starts to Read
Slightly more difficult words in simple sentences help new readers build confidence.

LEVEL 3

Your Child Reads with Help
More complex words and sentences and longer text lengths help young readers reach reading proficiency.

LEVEL 4

Your Child Reads Alone
Practicing difficult words and sentences brings independent readers to the next level: reading chapter books.

For Sterling and Heidi: extreme survivors
of adventurous childhoods. Carry on!

—C.R. and P.R.

Photo credits
Cover/jacket/title page: © Ken Lucas Inc/Visuals Unlimited/Corbis
4: (left) © Amee Cross/Shutterstock; (right) © Gentoo Multimedia Limited/Shutterstock; 5: (top) © John Downer/
Photolibrary/Getty Images; (bottom) © HamsterMan/Shutterstock; 6: © Benjamindewit/Shutterstock; 7: © BMJ/Shutterstock;
8: © AnimalsAnimals/SuperStock; 9: © Mary McDonald/Nature PictureLibrary; 10: © EastVillage Images/Shutterstock;
11: © Gary Yim/Shutterstock; 12: © A. Filis/Associated Press; 13: © Ralph White/Corbis; 14–15: © Science Picture Co./
Corbis; 16–17: © Reinhard Dirscherl/Alamy; 18–19: © Rob Fleming/Ardea; 20–21: © Juniors Bildarchiv GmbH Alamy;
22–23: © Eric Broder Van Dyke/Shutterstock; 23: (inset) © blickwinkel/Alamy; 24: © Stephane Bidouze/Shutterstock;
25: © Eric Isselee/Shutterstock; 26–27: © Tonybrindley/Dreamstime; 28–29: © Science PR/Oxford Scientific/Getty Images;
30–31 (left to right): Tick © Dariusz Majgier/Shutterstock, Brine Shrimp © blickwinkel/Alamy, Tubeworms © Ralph White/
Corbis, Peregrine Falcon © Mark Bridger/Shutterstock, Rattlesnake © Tom Reichner/Shutterstock, Watermelon Snow © Gary
Yim/Shutterstock, Blind Fish © Hamsterman/Dreamstime, Penguins © Gentoo Multimedia Limited/Shutterstock, Yeti Crab ©
A. Filis/Associated Press, Kangaroo Rat © Chappell, Mark/Animals Animals, Shoal of fish © Tammy616/iStockphoto,
Bar-headed goose © John Downer/Photolibrary/Getty Images, Sperm Whale © Shane Gross/iStockphoto, Arctic Tern © Sergey
Uryadnikov/Shutterstock, Morning Glory Pool © EastVillage Images/Shutterstock, Waterbear © Science PR/Oxford Scientific/
Getty Images, Polar Bear © City Escapes Nature Photography/Shutterstock; 32: © Chris Raxworthy

STERLING CHILDREN'S BOOKS
New York

An Imprint of Sterling Publishing
387 Park Avenue South
New York, NY 10016

STERLING CHILDREN'S BOOKS and the distinctive Sterling Children's Books logo
are trademarks of Sterling Publishing Co., Inc.

© 2014 by Sterling Publishing Co., Inc., and
The American Museum of Natural History

ISBN 978-1-4549-0631-5 (hardcover)
ISBN 978-1-4027-7791-2 (paperback)

Distributed in Canada by Sterling Publishing
c/o Canadian Manda Group, 165 Dufferin Street
Toronto, Ontario, Canada M6K 3H6
Distributed in the United Kingdom by GMC Distribution Services
Castle Place, 166 High Street, Lewes, East Sussex, England BN7 1XU
Distributed in Australia by Capricorn Link (Australia) Pty. Ltd.
P.O. Box 704, Windsor, NSW 2756, Australia

For information about custom editions, special sales, and premium and corporate purchases,
please contact Sterling Special Sales at 800-805-5489 or specialsales@sterlingpublishing.com.

Printed in China
Lot #:
2 4 6 8 10 9 7 5 3 1
01/14

www.sterlingpublishing.com/kids

FREE ACTIVITIES & PUZZLES ONLINE AT
http://www.sterlingpublishing.com/kids/sterlingeventkits

AMERICAN MUSEUM
OF NATURAL HISTORY

EASY READERS

EXTREME SURVIVORS

Connie and Peter Roop

STERLING CHILDREN'S BOOKS
New York

Rattlesnakes hunt in hot deserts.

Penguins live on ice.

Bar-headed geese fly very high.

Blind fish swim very deep.

These animals are extreme survivors.

They live where most humans cannot.

Let's see how some plants and

animals survive!

Polar bears live in the Arctic.

It is very cold there.

But polar bears have two layers of fur
to keep them warm.

Emperor penguins live in Antarctica.

It is an icy land.

Penguins have feathers and thick fat

to keep them warm.

Rattlesnakes and kangaroo rats live
in very hot, dry deserts.

Rattlesnakes keep cool by hiding
in holes.
They sip dew from rocks and plants.

Kangaroo rats also hide in holes.

They get water from seeds they eat.

Morning Glory Pool is a hot spring in Yellowstone National Park.

This pool is home to colorful bacteria.

This water is hot enough to cook an egg!

Pink algae live in snow and ice.
Snow with pink algae is called
watermelon snow. The pink color
protects algae from harmful light.

Few animals can live in the deep ocean.

There is no light there.

Deep ocean water is cold and heavy.

But in some places, hot water boils
out of vents in the ocean floor.
Yeti crabs and tubeworms find food
around these vents.

Blind fish swim inside caves.

These caves can be deep
underground.

Blind fish cannot see.

They find food by using touch
and smell.

Blind fish look pink from the blood
under their see-through skin.

Sperm whales dive 6,500 feet down

in the ocean.

That's over a mile!

They hunt deep in the ocean

for squid to eat.

Sperm whales can hold their breath

for over an hour.

Bar-headed geese fly high over the Himalayas.
The Himalayas are the world's tallest mountains.

Bar-headed geese fly higher than many airplanes!

How can a tiny fish get away from a hungry shark?

By swimming in a group!

Fish are hard to hunt when they are
in a group. These fish stay together
when a shark comes. That way, each
fish has a better chance to live.

This is the Great Salt Lake in Utah.

The water in this lake is twice as salty

as the ocean.

Brine shrimp live here.

Brine shrimp can survive well in super-salty water.
They can live in salt better than any other creature.

Ticks are skilled survivors.

They wait for just the right moment.

Then they jump onto the skin of

animals like deer and dogs.

These deer and dogs are called *hosts*.

Ticks drink their blood to survive.

This tick will drop off its dog host

when it is full.

Arctic terns travel farther than any other animal.

These birds fly between Antarctica and the Arctic to find food.

Arctic terns dive to catch fish to eat.

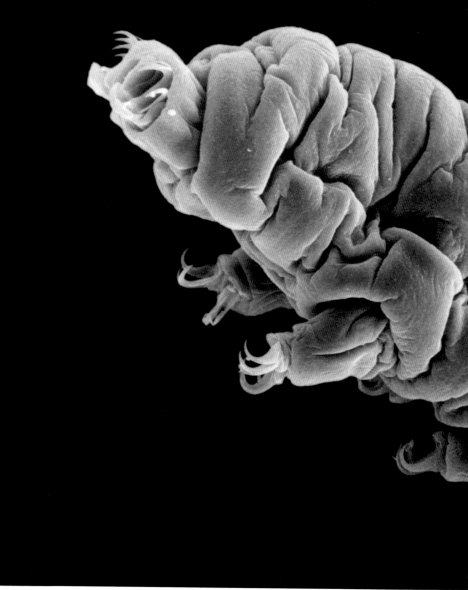

What is the most extreme survivor?

A water bear!

Water bears are so small, you need a microscope to see them.

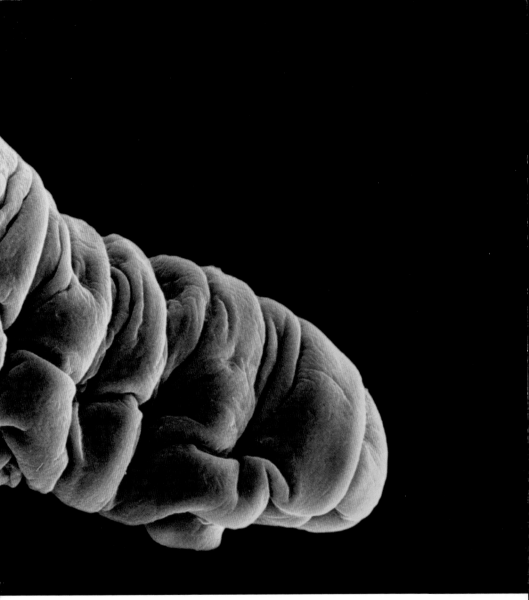

They can survive anywhere—even in space!

They can live at temperatures of

300° F or –327° F.

Now *that* is extreme!

High in the sky and deep

in the ocean . . .

In hot deserts and on cold ice . . .

In salty water and dark caves . . .

. . . animals and plants survive in Earth's most extreme places!

MEET THE EXPERT!

I am **Chris Raxworthy**, a herpetologist at the American Museum of Natural History. A herpetologist studies modern species of amphibians and reptiles. As a young boy I loved catching salamanders and frogs, and I still remember the first time I held a python; it was at a zoo when I was four. My pet tortoise, Persephone, still lives with me. I bought her in a pet shop in 1979. While I was at university in London, England, I studied zoology and learned about many extreme animals, like the ones you've just read about. Working at the American Museum of Natural History means I am always learning new and exciting things about our natural world.

My research includes exploring little-known tropical forests in Madagascar, Africa, and in the Indian Ocean. I look for new species of reptiles and amphibians, and I describe where and how to find them. Sometimes we walk for several days to reach a study area. My favorite reptiles are chameleons. More than half the world's species of chameleons are found only in Madagascar.

When I am back at the Museum, I use my field results, the research collections, and our laboratories to look at the form, genetics, and geographic locations of the animals I study. This helps us to protect rare species and better understand how these species evolved and what habitats they need. I also teach students, work on exhibitions, such as our exhibition *Frogs: A Chorus of Colors*, and help make all kinds of books, including this one!

7